TOUGHIE TOFFEE
A Collection of Citywise Poems

The world of the city with its parks, dogs,
laundrettes, canals, streets and schools is
conjured up in this lively collection of city-
wise poems from well known poets and from
new and exciting voices.

Other poetry collections published by Lions

Toughie Toffee

Citywise Poems
chosen by David Orme

Illustrated by
Martin Chatterton pages 8–51
Christine Roche pages 54–91
Jane Eccles pages 92–128

Lions

ACKNOWLEDGEMENTS

Individual poems in this collection © the authors 1989.

'I like this Town' by D. J. Enright first appeared in 'Rhyme Times Rhyme' (Collins) and is reproduced by permission of the author and Watson, Little Ltd. 'Bonfire Night and Mr Ellison' by Matt Simpson first appeared in 'Making Arrangements' (Bloodaxe Books Ltd). 'Laundrette' by Liz Lochhead first appeared in 'Dreaming Frankenstein' (Polygon Books). 'Hitting the Moon' by Phoebe Hesketh first appeared in 'A Song of Sunlight' (Chatto and Windus). 'At Night in the Laundrette' by Gerda Mayer first appeared in 'The Knockabout Show' (Chatto and Windus). 'Ducks Don't Shop in Sainsbury's' and 'My Dentist is a Rogue' by Gary Boswell first appeared in 'It's Brilliant' and are reproduced by permission of the author and Stride Publications. 'The Tidy Burglar' and 'Micky Hackett's Rocket' by Leo Aylen first appeared in 'Rhymoceros' (Macmillan). 'Leaving Home' by Sandra Mundel is published by permission of the author and BASCO.

A number of these poems first appeared in 'Poetry Express' published by the Schools Poetry Association.

The author wishes to acknowledge the generous help of Apples and Snakes.

First published in Great Britain 1989 by Lions
8 Grafton Street, London W1X 3LA

Lions is an imprint of
the Children's Division, part of
the Collins Publishing Group

Collection Copyright © David Orme
All rights reserved

Printed in Great Britain
by Wiliam Collins Sons & Co. Ltd, Glasgow

Contents

I like the town

D. J. Enright

Kids are supposed to like the country –
Because it is natural,
Like them.
And is made up of villages, small
Things, like them.

But I like the town,
With proper white faces
And no empty spaces
Filled with queer noises.

Not the big city,
For that's a pity!
Longwinded like London,
Tottery like Tokyo,
Panting like Paris,
Or choked like Chicago.

But a middling-sized town,
Roads going up,
Streets going down,
And people you know
And people you don't.
In short, just so.

Toughie Toffee

Paul Johnson

11

Streetwise
Irene Rawnsley

Beware of rats! Cool cats
are easy talkers, wearing
shady hats, collars

turned up high;
with sneaky cases bugged
for sound they'll try

to start conversations,
ask kind questions; be
wise to their devices;

Jump fast before they
play catch, these rats
are spies in cat disguises.

12

Rats

Tony Charles

Mum said the hall was draughty,
the ceilings too low,
back bedroom too small.
And Dad said the walls
weren't straight; and the lane was dirty:
I never noticed; it was just home.

And the lane-end had a brook
and a big hill
with black gravelly stuff that slithered you all
down one side.
Adults said it looked
like an old slag-heap – spoil showed still
where the grass hadn't grown.
They called it the Tip, but it was
    Kanchenjunga,
dangerous and rocky in Winter, a wide
waste with yetis; or, in Summer,
hot rocks with Indians who died
in thousands each day.

And the brook, they say,
is smelly, no fit place
for you to play in. Look! they say,
A rat's under the bridge there!
And, sure enough, a whiskered face
points out at me and, scared

13

by something, slips sleekly long-bodied
down through the furtive stream,
the water unmuddied
as the long tail trails
ripples behind it.

And you mustn't mind it if I dream
of those forbidden rats, and build
dams out of mud, to bale
the water into new-dug channels;
for my canals
carry great ships all round the world,
and mutineers are killed,
strange ports are sighted, slaves disembark
with sea-chests full of gold.

And have I told you?
Graham Cashmore's got a new flat
the other side of the park;
it's got its own lift
and boxes downstairs for the post
and a balcony, with stranglers and ghosts
making the curtains shift . . .
But he hasn't got any rats.

The hat
Gerda Mayer

He only wears it when it rains.
The hat
turns him into a rat.

His face peaks
beneath the narrow brown brim.
The hat swallows him up;

And turns him into
a bit-part crook;
into a Hollywood gangster;
into the man who works
for the Big Bad Boss.

If the rain doesn't stop soon,
there'll be a shoot-out.

Ducks don't shop in Sainsbury's

Gary Boswell

You can't get millet at Sainsbury's
and they don't sell grass or weed
it's a total dead loss
for heather and moss
and they don't stock sunflower seed.

They've got some fish in the freezer
but they're low on rats and mice
and you're out of luck
if you're a debonair duck
and you want to buy something nice

'cos none of their bread is stale
and they've stopped selling hay and straw.
Let's face it, if you were a duck in Sainsbury's,
you'd be heading for the exit door!

The gourmets
John Cotton

The Rovers have won, it is Saturday night
And Ginger and me are feeling quite bright.
We're both growing lads so we need lots of
    nosh
So we go in for quantity rather then posh.
So after our tea of eggs and boiled ham,
Fried bread and toast with lashings of jam,
It's off to the Pie Shop for Joe's mushy peas
Which we help to wash down with several teas.
Then it's round to the "Indian" for a quick
    vindaloo
With chappaties and dhall with Mr Chindoo.
We drop into the pub to wish our friend cheers
And take in pork scratchings and couple of
    beers.
Time now for the "Chinese" with bean shoots
    and spring rolls
Which we eat with soy sauce from dragony
    bowls.
At the Dona-Kebab, in a van round the corner,
We eat skewers of meat which makes us feel
    warmer
Both inside and out, but we have to be nippy
To get to "Aunt May's" before she closes the
    Chippy!
There some cod and a bagfull of chips set us up
Before stopping at Sam's for a wedge and a cup

Of hot cocoa at his all-night under-arch stall.
"Any more?" asks Sam. "Thanks, that just about
  all"
We say as we go home, feeling all right
Having eaten our way through Saturday night.

A bellyful
John C. Desmond

Fred's fisheries
serve up
real portions.
Ordering cod,
chips and peas
they came on
three separate plates.

After two mouthfuls
I came across
this pair of boots.
Carefully clearing
the way I called
"Is anyone there?"

18

As the echo

died away
a distant voice
replied "Thank God.
Is that daylight?"

"Can I help?"

"Yes, but first
'phone the wife."

"What name?"

"Just tell her
you've found
Jonah."

The song of the homeworkers
Trevor Millum

**To be read or chanted with
increasing velocity**

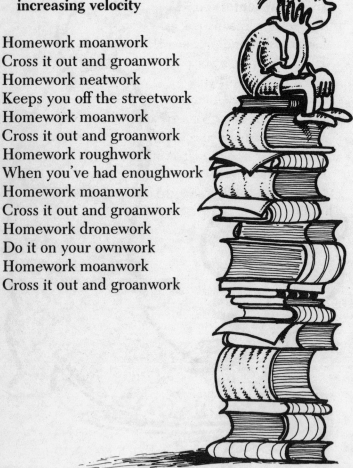

Homework moanwork
Cross it out and groanwork
Homework neatwork
Keeps you off the streetwork
Homework moanwork
Cross it out and groanwork
Homework roughwork
When you've had enoughwork
Homework moanwork
Cross it out and groanwork
Homework dronework
Do it on your ownwork
Homework moanwork
Cross it out and groanwork

Homework gloomwork
Gaze around the roomwork
Homework moanwork
Cross it out and groanwork
Homework guesswork
Book is in a messwork
Homework moanwork
Cross it out and groanwork
Homework rushwork
Do it on the buswork
Homework moanwork
Cross it out and groanwork
Homework hatework
Hand your book in latework
Homework moanwork
Cross it out and groan groan GROANWORK

Good girls
Irene Rawnsley

Good girls
will always go like clockwork
home from school,

through the iron gates
where clambering boys
whisper and pull,

past houses
where curtains twitch
and a fingery witch beckons,

by the graveyard
where stone angels stir,
itching their wings,

past tunnelled woods
where forgotten wolves wait
for prey,

past dens
and caves and darknesses
they go like clockwork;

and when they come
to school again
their homework's done.

Computer compatible cat
Mike Johnson

Computer compatible cat
knew his way round the automat

that's why this cat is fat

    pressed the keys one by one
    select-a-dish
                then had some fun

    stretched out beneath the sun

No need to go fishing and freeze
risk his life by climbing trees
machines fulfilled each wish
no need for him to say please
just lift the latch and snatch the fish

tench and roach perch or plaice
this cat just loved to stuff his face

ate cod or carp as if in a race

But our friend made a mistake
mmm exotic fish not dace or hake

into his works cat threw a spanner

pressed the keys that spelt
PIRANHA

That's my dog!
Joan Poulson

Mum took me to the Dogs' Home
on my birthday. I'd waited
years, it seemed, for the day
to arrive. We went inside.

There were dogs of all sizes –
long-eared and short, in every
dog-colour you'd imagine. They
jumped up at the wire, barking
a plea "Choose me to take
home! Choose me! Take me!"
All of them, that is, but one.

They were lively, bright-eyed
with wagging tails that said
"It's *me* you want beside you
when you go for walks, to lie
next to your bed, protect you
in the park. *I'll* be your
mate, search your room before
you go in when it's dark."
All of them, that is, but him.

He lay watching from the back
of the run, black ears
drooped over big brown eyes
shivering, afraid, half the
size of any of the others.

Then I saw on his face
that look I knew from
my mirror – look that says
"I'm quiet, not brave, nothing
special in any way. But I'm
stronger than I seem, would
love to have a friend, someone
I can trust. I'd gladly share in
bad days – and make others full
of fun." I winked at him, grinned
up at Mum. And firmly said
"That's my dog! That's the one!"

Dog-gone
Russell Adams

There's a phantom dog in the city.
He never can be found.
We only know he's been here,
By the messages left around.

No one ever admits it
No one cleans it up.
But everybody steps right in.
This mess of a miscreant pup.

It always seems to happen,
Whenever you buy new shoes.
It squelches over the edges,
And packs hard into the grooves!

No matter how hard you scrape them,
Along the pavement side.
The smell goes with you all the day,
Like something nasty died!

Joggers, walkers, victims all,
Shout "It's a disgrace!"
Somewhere sits the phantom pooch,
With a smirk across his face.

Andrew's mother

Brian Moses

Andrew's mother
is fat & forty & whacks him
round the ears
when he doesn't hear her call.
She bawls at him to come in
at night,
& her son bawls back that he'll come
when he's had
just one more bat.
Till moments later
she breaks up the game,
shouldering past
like a skilled scrum-half,
moving in
like some heavyweight champ
holding on where no holds
are allowed . . .
Till fixing her lad
in a swift arm lock,
she rocks side to side
as they move through the alley,
past neighbours who gather by gates
to watch the fray . . .
And it makes Andrew mad
to be treated the way she treats
his dad!

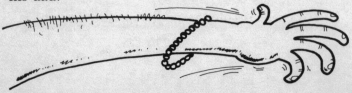

A listen to this
John Rice

A listen to this:

B fore we rush into anything, said the father, I'll

C you in the living room to

D side what to do about Tom's pocket money – and no

E can't have the car tonight –

F you no sense at all, he'll crash it!

G I never thought of that, said the mother, it's the

H old problem though; just how do you deal with a teenager.

I don't know what's best.

J in, day out I try to come up with a solution: well O

K I say to myself, what the

L should I care!

M not a psychiatrist!

N again Tom's not such a bad lad.

O you really think so? replied the father.

P ping Tom listened to all this at the window, waiting for his

Q to burst in on the conversation.

R you two serious, he yelled at his parents, growing up isn't easy

S pecially at my age!

T or coffee Tom, asked his mother politely.

U can't be serious, tea and coffee – is there no fizzy lemonade?

V for Espana! exclaimed his father lapsing into Spanish.

W strength and double your health said his mother

X why you should eat up your food and drink up your drinks.

Y can't you try to understand, I'm a teenager, that's all, enough

Z.

My dentist is a rogue
Gary Boswell

The waiting room has walls of cardboard
next to which us patients sit
and talk for a while about the weather
then shake in our shoes a bit

We sit there and we hear it
We sit there and we fear it
Even Roger Timminson's Dad
Every single one of us
must be a little bit mad

Chorus
aaaaaaaaaaaargyeeeeeeeeeeeeeeeeeeooww
   he's pulled her tongue out by mistake
ooooooooooooooooooooodescreeeeecheerrr
     his framed certificate it's a fake
aaaaaaaaaaaaaaaaqaaaademeneleyeerrrrrr
   he's poured that pink drink down her ear
oooooooooooooooooootymarblackberryyy
   quick, let's get out of here!!

He's been to court ten times this year
ten patients tried to sue him
one angry woman put him in a casserole
  – she tried to stew him!

Me dad went down to get a new crown
and unmangle the pain in his head
he expected to come away with a set of pearly
    whites
he got a mouth full of lead instead

Chorus:
aaaaaaaaaaaargyeeeeeeeeeeeeeeeeooww
he's pulled her tongue out by mistake
oooooooooooooooooooodescreeeeecheerrr
    his framed certificate it's a fake
aaaaaaaaaaaaaaaaqaaaademeneleyeerrrrrr
    he's poured that pink drink down her ear
oooooooooooooooooootymarblackberryyy
    quick, let's get out of here!!

The haunted lift
James Kirkup

On the ground floor
of this ultramodern
tower block

in the dead
middle
of the night

the lift doors
open, with a
clang.

Nobody enters,
and nobody
comes out.

In the dead
middle
of the night

the lift doors
close with a clang,
and the lift begins

to move
slowly
up –

with nobody in it,
nobody but
the ghost of a girl

who lived here once
on the thirteenth floor of
this ultramodern tower block.

One day, she went to play
in an old part of town,
and never came back.

She said she was just
going to the corner shop,
but she never came home.

Now her ghost
keeps pressing
in the dead

middle of the night
the button
for the thirteenth floor.

But when the door
opens with a clang
she cannot step out.

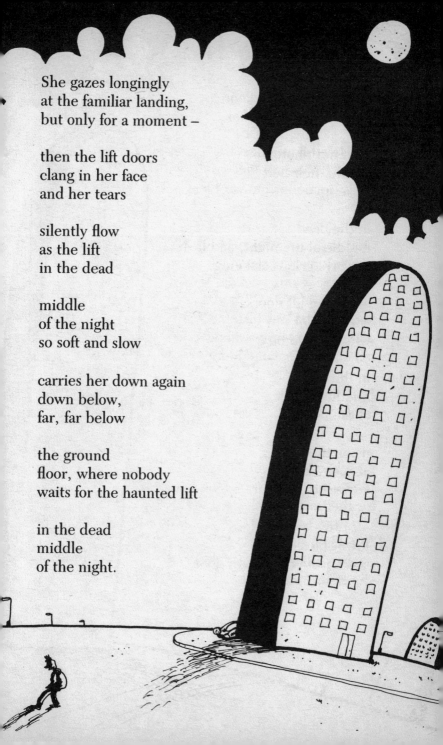

She gazes longingly
at the familiar landing,
but only for a moment –

then the lift doors
clang in her face
and her tears

silently flow
as the lift
in the dead

middle
of the night
so soft and slow

carries her down again
down below,
far, far below

the ground
floor, where nobody
waits for the haunted lift

in the dead
middle
of the night.

Sometimes
on the thirteenth floor
her mother and father

with her photo
beside their bed
wake up

in the dead
middle of the night, and hear
the mysterious clanging

of closing lift doors,
and wonder
who it could be

in the dead
middle
of the night

using the lift
at such
an unearthly hour.

– In this ultramodern
tower block
there is no thirteenth floor.

Bobs
Barry Heath

Bobs shop warrutend on
ower street
y'dint semucha obob cos
isnam keptit
wiusta asker f'twopenith
awohtyurantgot
an she weṇt't'look
forrit

meun ower lezwuns ast
er f'twopennuth othat
rahnd back
an she went't'look forrit
lez reached ower cahnta
an shicumback an seed
isfingus ona barrachoclut
shisez, "wot'y'dooin?"
and lez sez, "Ahm justonninit
rahnd sohzahcun read it!"

Candy
Dave Ward

Candy likes lollipops and bullseyes and
    bubblegum.
Candy likes sherbet and liquorice whirls.
    Where can she
get them? Where is she going? She won't tell
    anyone –
only Candy knows.

The sunlight sparkles on the street like icing
    sugar.
Candy dances down the pavement, trying to
    dodge the cracks.
One step, two step, hop and twirl. One jump
    forward and
two turns back.

Then Candy treads on a crack – and with a
    creaking, crumbling
crash, the street splits open, a kaleidescope of
    colour,
the street splits open as the sky turns round.
    Out of the
ground, out of the emptiness, Candy screams
    as the pink
lizard crawls.

Like a hot-water bottle filled with custard, a
    slithering mass

of wobbling blancmange. Candy screams again
    as it keeps on
coming, uttering a green sick groaning sound.

"Give me strawberry shortcake," the pink lizard
    wheezes.
"Give me lemon cheese," as it oozes on and on.

"I haven't got any," Candy whispers.
"Not even a bit of cinder toffee or a penny
    chew."

Candy cries, whimpering and wailing, but the
    lizard gets
bigger as it drinks all her tears, the lizard gets
    bigger
as it nibbles at her toes.

It slobbers, it gurgles, it splutters, and
    explodes!
Candy jumps back, never minding the cracks.
    Candy jumps
back as the lizard explodes.

Filling the street with sweets.
Filling the street with sweets. A rainbow lights
    the sky
as a litter of glittering wrappers comes drifting
    down
like snow.

Candy grabs them, giggling and grinning,
    ripping them open
to see what's inside. And what is inside, as she
    tears at
every wrapper? – a little pink lizard, drooling
    and slurping,
a little pink lizard, winking up at her, gurgling
    and snuffling
and blinking its eyes.

Amusements
Mango Chutney

Come in off the street, kids,
To Sid's arcade of fun,
Put your money in the slot,
Fire a laser gun,
Try and make your fortune with
Poker or pontoon,
Zap an alien or fly
A shuttle to the Moon.

Come and try your luck, kids,
a penny or a quid,
It's money in the bank for
Honest Uncle Sid.

He's got some one arm bandits,
They'll really make your day,
Just HOLD that pair of strawberries
That's the way to make 'em pay,
Three bells, or grapes, or oranges,
A winning line! And then
The ten P coins come pouring out

And you put them in again.

Come and try your luck, kids,
A penny or a quid,
It's money in the bank for
Honest Uncle Sid.

Try cascading pennies,
They'll really drive you mad,
You think your coin is bound to score,
But kiddies, you've been had,
For now and then, he'll let you win,
For Sid's a decent bloke;
But his machines so tantalise

You'll stay until you're broke.

Come and try your luck, kids,
A penny or a quid,
It's money in the bank for
Honest Uncle Sid.

Old Mister Roberts
Tony Charles

Old Mister Roberts lives on the corner
next to the sweetshop. Tall and dusty,
very slow-moving; walks with a cane.
Thin dry face, all stretched and bony,
straight pinched nose with bristly whiskers,
not much hair, but bushy eyebrows,
small blue eyes as bright as flames.

Old Mister Roberts goes out walking;
raises his hat if you say Good Morning,
shakes his stick if you call him names.
Always wears an old red waistcoat,
jacket patched with leather elbows,
wears no collar when it's sunny,
wears a trilby when it rains.

Old Mister Roberts was a sailor:
round the world with coal and timber
– probably sailed the Spanish Main.
Sometimes, in the park in Summer,
you can meet him when he's walking;
then he'll sit and tell you stories,
dreaming that he's young again.

Bomblast!

Peter Dixon

Bomblast! Bomblast! Come on out!
That's what all the children shout.
Bomblast! Bomblast! One, two, three
Bomblast! Bomblast! Can't catch me!

Bomblast! Bomblast! Kick his door!
Said he was a soldier in 1944 . . .
Said he was a gunner in a place called France . . .
Rattle on his door-knob and watch him dance!

Said he was a soldier in the King's Grenadiers.
Said he'd been a prisoner and fought for years.
Said he'd been a sergeant, said he'd fought the
    hun.
Said he'd fought with hand-grenade,
    with bayonet, blade and gun.

Said he'd been a hero.
Said he'd saved men's lives.
And now he lives in Stanley Street
At number fifty five.

He's old and worn and grumpy.
His eyes are black and sad.
He never cleans his windows
And the big boys say he's mad.

So it's *Up and In and at him!*
And it's *Kick and knock and run!*
And it's *Catch us Mr Bomblast!*
Catch us if you can!

So it's *Bomblast! Bomblast! One, two, three*
Bomblast! Bomblast!

what's a V.C.?

Lost

Irene Rawnsley

"This is the key
that opens the door
of the house on the street
where I live.

These are the shoes
that walked to the shop
but won't take me back
to the house on the street
where I live.

This is the pension
in my purse
inside the bag
that goes with the shoes
that won't walk back
to the house on the street
where I live."

Here's the policeman
tall and kind
knows Mrs Edgerton's
uncertain mind;

Carries her bag
and takes her arm,
leads her home
to the house on the street
where she lives.

Here's the report
that he makes at the station;
"Area due for demolition
but she won't move.
She's the last one left
in a house on the street
where she lives".

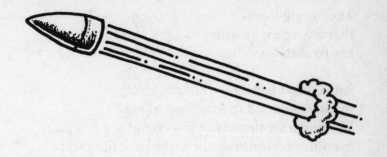

Don't you know there's a war on?
Brian Moses

My mother didn't know there was a war on!
She hung out her washing on the line
as I crouched among the cabbages
and gave covering fire.

My father didn't know there was a war on!
He called out "Hello" as he came in from work
& I broke cover, shouted back,
ignoring the cracking of bullets.

The dog didn't know there was a war on!
He carried on sniffing in No Man's Land
then cocked a leg on the sign I'd painted
to warn of the danger from mines.

The neighbours didn't know there was a war
    on!
They hung over our fence & complained
that one of my missiles went A.W.O.L.
& drove its way through the dahlias.

After that I jacked in the war,
ran up a white flag & agreed to end
hostilities for the day. I pulled out my troops
from the flower beds, brought back the dead
to life, then boxed them all & went indoors.

There wasn't much for tea & when
I complained Mum snapped, "I thought you
    said
there's a war on, & how am I supposed
to bring supplies through a battle zone?"

Later I watched the News on T.V.
It seemed there was a war on everywhere.
Perhaps I'll declare an outbreak of peace
    tomorrow!

Bonfire Night and Mr Ellison
Matt Simpson

On the bombed side of the street,
before they plonked those shoe-box prefabs
    down,
we raised our bonfire, roofing it
with planks we'd nicked from Barney's Yard.
And when night came and we were still
awake in all its wickedness,
we prodded rolled newspaper torches in
between the planks to let the fire rip.

But in the awe of it, the hush,
we heard the Elloes' drunken father curse
and clatter like a one-man-band
along the street. And next,
the pistol shot of a slammed front door,
his whingeing wife,
thin as a needle, quick as a pain,
dragging off four yapping dogs of sons
around the foundry corner
and away up Knowsley Road.

No-one called me in. I was left
with a bonfire playing merry hell
with the dark, while half-seas Mr Ellison,
tottering like a bull come round
from surgery, hauled out and flung
curtains, chairs, and table legs
among the splintering flames. And moved
by generosity: "There's something
for your bommy, Matt."

Finally the sideboard's bulk.
But halfway across the cobbled street
strength and fury failed. "I'll have
a bloody bommy by meself," he said,
striking matches into drawers.

Just two of us, alone, with darkness winning:
me not twelve years old, and him
slumped on the kerbstones, blubbering.

Three witches
dave calder

three witches met in back canning street
howling this song, stamping their feet:

"bad to worse, bad to worse
    children scream and mothers curse
    broken bottles, lumps of brick,
    pools of water thick with oil-slick,
    sludge of drain and sick of cat,
    brown spittle that some thick lad spat,
    gunge of grease and gob of tar,
    odd rusted bits off burnt-out cars;
    across the slimy pavingstones
    smear curry chips and chicken bones,
    snotty tissues, smelly rags,
    torn-up slug-stained plastic bags,
    and to make sure the spell succeeds
    throw in a mattress full of fleas
    that smells so bad that rats won't eat it
    and leave it to rot – the spells completed.
    grouse and grump, grouse and grump,
this street has turned
                    into
                    a dump

51

Y.T.S.
Terry Caffrey

Strong arms – strong thighs head strong street
  wise,
Mind your car Mr Mr mind your car?
and say no if you dare
and we promise you sir
you'll have a scratch and a dent
and a bumper bar bent
and a wiper arm torn
and a played out horn
a car with no sense
but plenty of vents.
Mind your car
Mr Mr mind your car.

Photo by Gary Boswe

Medallion man rap
Martin Glynn

You can see him around
Everywhere
He's got trendy clothes
And super slick hair
A super large ego
That's part of his plan
The name of this thing
Is medallion man!!

He's got gold on his fingers
Gold round his neck
Every type of gold
He respects
He worships just money
He tries to be flash
All for the sake of
Cash!!
Where does he get his money from
nobody knows
His vast collection
Just grows and grows
Try to understand
As best as you can
That's the way of life
For medallion man!!

When he goes out
He has to look cool
Looks down on the people
Tries to make us look fool
By flashin
His jewelry
To try and show his
Superiority
He wants all of us to be his fan
That son of a bitch
Medallion man

But jewelry alone
Is not enuff
So he finds a woman
As part of his bluff
To match his image
She has to be slick

With make-up mask
And ego trip
She's riding in his
New reg car
He feels he is a superstar
He goes around with a clan
That's what you need
To be medallion man

But
Hear me now
And hear me good
Get it straight
And understood
We fought a black struggle
To remove the chain
Now you've put it back on
Just to be vain
You wear your wealth
Just for show
While oppression for our people
Grows and grows
Conchusness inside
Your ass

Brains between your legs
That's all you'll pass
How many black people
Have been sold
To cater for
Your love of gold
So medallion man
You're nothing great
Your minds mixed up
In a terrible state
Out of all the people
You have used
You've lied and cheated
And abused
It's only for a time
A short life span
Cause you're goin
Nowhere but down

**MEDALLION
MAN**

Swap? Sell? Small ads sell fast
Trevor Millum

1950 Dad. Good runner; needs one or
Two repairs; a few grey hairs but
Nothing a respray couldn't fix
Would like a 1966 five speed turbo
In exchange: something in the sporty
Twin-carb range.

1920s Granny. Not many like this
In such clean and rust free state.
You must stop by to view! All chrome
As new, original fascia retained
Upholstery unstained. Passed MOT
Last week: will only swap for some-
Thing quite unique.

1986 low mileage Brother. As eco-
Nomical as any other. Must mention
Does need some attention. Stream-
Lined, rear spoiler. Runs on milk
Baby oil and gripe water. Serviced;
Needs rear wash/wipe. Only one
Owner; not yet run in. Will swap
For anything.

City jungle
Pie Corbett

Rain splinters town.

Lizard cars cruise by;
their radiators grin.

Thin headlights stare –
shop doorways keep
their mouths shut.

At the roadside
hunched houses cough.

Newspapers shuffle by,
hands in their pockets.
The gutter gargles.

A motorbike snarls;
Dustbins flinch.

Streetlights bare
their yellow teeth.
The motorway's
cat-black tongue
lashes across
the glistening back
of the tarmac night.

The Tracy Morgan gang
Leo Aylen

1.
"Tracy Morgan's tied 'er pigtails wiv baconrind.
Poowee! How disgustin'."

Tracy says that what she's tied 'er pigtails with
Is a shoelace she took from 'er little brother.
And she says 'e's disgustin'.
'Cause if it still looks like baconrind –
That proves 'e didn't polish 'is shoes this
     morning!

So poowee to you!

2.
"Tracy Morgan's duffle-coat
Is spattered with blood."

Tracy says it's 'cause she wrapped her little
     brother up
When 'e was cut.

"Who cut him, Tracy?"
                              "Well . . . me . . .
                              like . . .
We was playin' 'uman sacrifice
Wiv the knife for peelin' carrots."

Kevin, blood stainin' 'is new yellow shirt,
'As just shot Sharon wiv 'is bow-an'-arrer.

3.
"Tracy Morgan's plannin' to murder
All the boys in the world."

"And where's Kevin?"

Tracy says she's vowed to have revenge on
     Trevor,
'Cause 'e wouldn't kiss 'er be'ind the rabbit
     'utches . . .
And then 'e put a plastic dog-do
In 'er chocolate pudding.

"'Ow you goin' to kill us, Trace?"

"By the power of my will.
Like I killed Kevin,
'Cause 'e keeps on usin'
My banana-flavoured toothpaste."

"Is that your evil eye then, Trace?
I call it squintin'."

Kevin came in soon after break.
'E was sick on the plasticine model prehistoric
    village.

Under questionin' by teach
'E broke down and confessed
'Ow Tracy'd given 'im seventeen packs
Of Smarties to stay 'ome.

"When I commit murder," said the Head,
Twanging his purple braces,
"You can be sure . . . haw-haw, haw-haw . . .
That I shall leave no . . . traces!!"

Frank
Colin West

We don't mention Frank
In this house any more;
No, not since he nailed
Mother's boots to the floor.
What makes matters worse
With regard to this crime
Is Mother was wearing
Her boots at the time.

Sight Test
Rose Sutherland

The Meat Boutique

Nick Toczek

WITH THE CHIC FREAK CLIQUE FROM THE MEAT BOUTIQUE
you wake in bacon, shave in gravy, take a wash in warm goulash
hit the street in a suit of meat 'n' knock 'em flat in your porkpie hat

THEN...
WHAM! BAM!
BEEF 'N' LAMB
MUTTON yr BUTTON
'N' STEW yr SHOE

A D V E R T I S E M E N T

feel fresh as flesh
with T.W.I.C.E the charm
try Gammon roll-on underarm!

GOD DAMN
VEAL 'N' HAM
WALK 'N' TALK
AS SUAVE AS PORK

A D V E R T I S E M E N T

life is easy, bright and breezy
when you make your skin go greasy.
DON'T BE A DRIP IN DRIPPING.
DON'T BE A PRAT IN FAT.
It's LARD, LARD for the lad who's hard!
If it ain't lard it's LAH-DI-DAH!"

SO
SLAM! BLAM!
BRAWN 'N' SPAM
SURLOIN STEAK 'N'
STREAKY BACON
WHAM! BAM!
BEEF 'N' LAMB
MUTTON yr BUTTON
'N' STEW yr SHOE
GOD DAMN!
VEAL 'N' HAM
WALK 'N' TALK
AS SUAVE AS PORK..!

KaZAM! Unique, sleek at their peak
they're the chic, freak clique
the chic, freak clique
from the meat Boutique

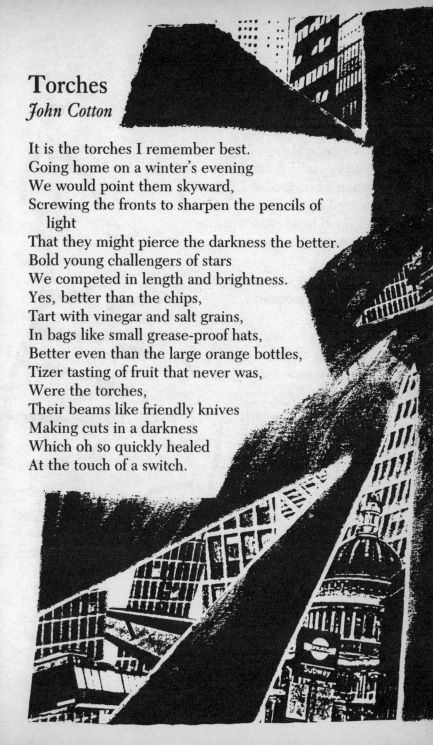

Torches
John Cotton

It is the torches I remember best.
Going home on a winter's evening
We would point them skyward,
Screwing the fronts to sharpen the pencils of
    light
That they might pierce the darkness the better.
Bold young challengers of stars
We competed in length and brightness.
Yes, better than the chips,
Tart with vinegar and salt grains,
In bags like small grease-proof hats,
Better even than the large orange bottles,
Tizer tasting of fruit that never was,
Were the torches,
Their beams like friendly knives
Making cuts in a darkness
Which oh so quickly healed
At the touch of a switch.

Fisherman's tale
Irene Rawnsley

By the canal
I was quietly fishing
when a bowler hat
floated by,
stopped level with my eye
and began to rise.

Below it was a man's head
wearing spectacles;
he asked,
"This way to Brackley?"
"Straight ahead."
The face sank back

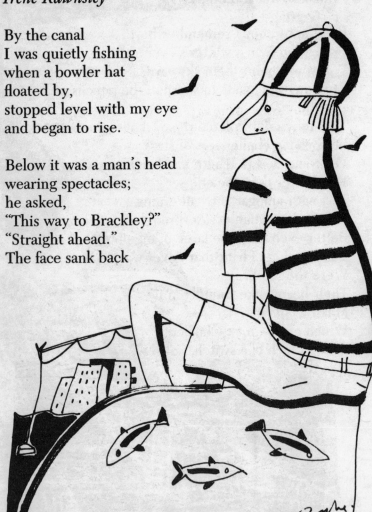

beneath the wet,
but I was thinking
Brackley's seven miles,
it's getting late;
perhaps he doesn't know
how far.

I tapped the hat
with my rod; again
the face rose; "Yes?"
"You'll need to hurry
to arrive before dark."
"Don't worry," he said;
I'm on my bike."

Passers-by

Colin West

A passer-by
Was passing by
A bypass,
And passing by
The bypass,
A passer-by
Passed by;
By passing by
A bypass
As a passer-by
Passed by,

A passer-by
Was passed by
By a bypass
Passer-by.

The revenge of Catford Lil
Mango Chutney

There's a seedy Chinese takeaway to the north
   of Finsbury Square,
There's a grubby little bedsit in East Penge,
There's a woman who is still described as
   Catford Lil,
And here's a tale of Catford Lil's revenge.

Our grubby bedsit dweller was a fine
   upstanding feller
Whose Christian name was William – call him Bill,
At the time that I'm relating no woman was he
   dating
For he'd lost his heart and soul to Catford Lil.

"Oh Lilly! Dearest Lilly! I think I'm going silly,
I can think of nothing else but loving you;
And yet you spurn my charms, will not have
   me in your arms,
Oh Lilly! I'd do anything for you!"

"Anything?" she said, and as she hadn't fed,
She revealed to Bill the means to have his way.
"I am starving, Billy Darling, so show me that
   you love me,
By getting me a Chinese takeaway."

"Two portions of fried rice, some spare ribs
   would be nice,

69

some chicken and some prawn balls sweet and sour,
Fetch me this and I'll be true, and surely marry you,
But I want my dinner here within the hour.

"Now I don't want food from Woo, Chang's
    takeaway won't do,
On Chinese food I'm most particulaire,
So get my little treat – it's the only food I'll eat,
From the takeaway that's north of Finsbury square."

She was fed up with him doing all the writing
    and the wooing,
and ringing up and following her about.
She could have simply said, "dear Billy, please
    drop dead,"
But she thought this little scheme would sort
    him out.

But off poor Billy went; he'd have to spend his rent,
On finding Lil the sort of grub she'd like;
He'd no money for a bus, or a taxi or the tube,
He'd have to go like lightning on his bike.

And so our lovestruck lad went off peddling like mad
To the Chinese takeaway near Finsbury Square,
It was half an hour to get there, five minutes in
    the shop,
And back with only moments left to spare.

That ride had done for Bill; he was feeling
    rather ill;

He'd paid the price for being far too nippy,
But despite his cycling skill, there was no sign
    of heartless Lil;
She'd run off with Ron Jenkins from the chippy.

And that was Lil's revenge. Bill retired to East
    Penge,
And found himself a grubby bedsit, where,
He thought of Sweet Lil's hips – now grown fat
    with Ronnie's chips –
And of his love – turned sour with despair.

Biking free
Pie Corbett

Black tyres spin –
pattern's tread –
spokes flicker –
legs of lead.

Steel rim squeals –
brake blocks clasp –
squeeze as hard –
as a bully's grasp.

Streets blur by –
eyeball stings –
handles gleam –
cycle sings.

Pounding pulse –
heart beats' race –
clicking gears –
furious pace.

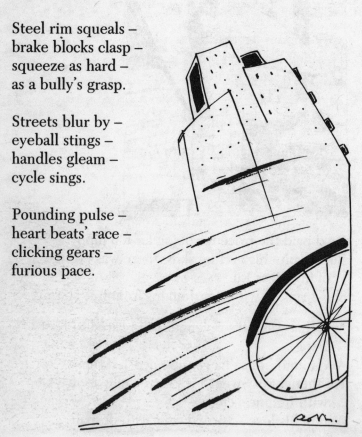

Hitting the moon
Phoebe Hesketh

I'm Rodney on my red-hot motor-bike
roaring between hedges,
ripping the air like calico,
rattling angrier bullets
than machine-guns as I go.

My armour against the world
is shiny black and white plastic.
Zipped inside my black jacket
no one can reach me;
under my white helmet
I'm not afraid any more.
The speed-needle flicks to ninety;
curves race around me
hugging my flight
from narrow streets, hindering traffic,
restrictions and family rows.

On my pulsing hot-blood
motor-bike
I'm Rodney new-made –
more than a boy, more
than a man,
unafraid of the world I conquer –
lashing out the miles, leaning
on the wind, learning
how it feels to be hitting the
moon.

Asleep or awake
James Kirkup

When everyone's asleep at home,
what's going on in the streets outside?
On my dresser the tidy's brush and comb
look into the mirror that tries to hide
(with the curtains drawn on the windowpanes)
the secret life of shunting trains
as they whistle forlornly through the dark,
like the hooting of ships putting out to sea
while the lighthouse beam crashes through the
    park
and the wind strips the leaves from bush
    and tree.

And if there's a moon, the shadows it casts
are different from any we know by day:
in the harbour, the sailing ships' rocking masts
stretch and swing with a phantom sway,
throwing mad shapes on the ebbing tide
while the dockyards' iron skeletons ride
like death-ships on the darkling waves,
and crosses are black in the churchyard walls
like vampires hoisting themselves from their
    graves –
and out of the thatch a barn-owl calls.

– Is it only in dreams we seem to meet
burglars and murderers running away,
or the tramp of an army's marching feet
off to the wars of another day?
O, out in the streets where nobody goes
the buildings look strange in their moonlit
    rows,
and their windows look down like big dark eyes
on our house, where curtains and blinds are
    drawn,
so they cannot see in – where each one lies
asleep (or awake) till the break of dawn.

A short cut . . . after dark
Wes Magee

It's late.
The night is icy
as we head for home
after carol singing,
coins chinking in our collecting tin.
It's so cold.
Our fingers feel frost-bitten.
The estate is quiet,
there's no one about.
Snow lies on the pavement.
Far away a dog barks.

It's late.
We decide to take a short cut
through the school grounds.
So, climb the wall, drop,
and race past the "No Trespassers' sign,
race past the skeletal trees,
the bushes hunched
like sleeping bears.
Beneath our Wellingtons
the crisp snow creaks.
So dark, so dark.

It's late.
Hearts thumping,
we stop, breathless,

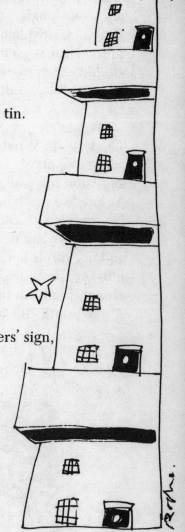

77

at the school building.
We inhale fast
and the freezing air
hurts our lungs.
Listen! An owl hoots.
In the clear sky a million stars
are like silver nails hammered into the hull
of a vast, black ship.

It's late.
The last lap. Wraith-like we skate
across the playground
and vault the padlocked gate.
At last, we reach our street.
No cars. No people.
Three days before Christmas
and our carols long gone
into the frozen night.
Home. Lights in the hall.
Warmth. It's late.

Establishment
Colin West

Let's all go to the establishment!
Let's all go to what establishment?
Let's all go to the establishment with automatic
   washing machines!
*Let's all go to the establishment with automatic
   washing machines for whose use?*

Let's all go to the establishment with automatic
   washing machines for public use!
No thanks, I must go to the laundrette . . .

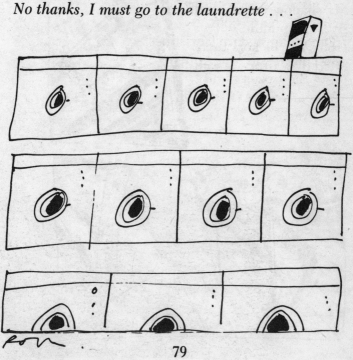

At night in the laundrette
Gerda Mayer

I sit in the laundrette
Watch my reflection sitting
On the chequered pavement

The black wet street reflects
Moonmilk, primroses
A bus sails by, a boat
Festooned with lanterns

My shadow warms itself
By a red puddle
Hell's fire flickers there
Stirred by drops of rain

Laundrette
Liz Lochhead

We sit nebulous in steam.
It calms the air and makes the windows stream
rippling the hinterland's big houses to a blur
of bedsits – not a patch on what they were before.

We stuff the tub, jam money in the slot,
sit back on rickle chairs not
reading. The paperbacks in our pockets curl.
Our eyes are riveted. Our own colours whirl.

We pour in smithereens of soap. The machine sobs
through its cycle. The rhythm throbs
and changes. Suds drool and slobber in the churn
Our duds don't know which way to turn.

The dark shoves one man in,
lugging a bundle like a wandering Jew. Linen
washed in public here.
We let out of the bag who we are.

This youngwife has a fine stack of sheets, each pair
a present. She admires their clean cut air
of colourschemes and being chosen. Are the
   dyes fast?
This christening lather will be the first test.

This woman is deadpan before the rinse and sluice

of the family in a bagwash. Let them stew in
   their juice
to a final fankle, twisted, wrung out into rope,
hard to unravel. She sees a kaleidoscope

For her to narrow her eyes and blow smoke at,
   his overalls
and pants ballooning, tangling with her smalls
and the teeshirts skinned from her wriggling son.
She has a weather eye for what might shrink or run.

This dour man does for himself. Before him,
half lost, his small possessions swim.
Cast off, random
they nose and nudge the porthole glass like
   flotsam.

Miss Hubbard
Peter Dixon

She's at the window again!
Bug eyed,
Dressing gowned, and grey.
"See her!" squeal the Brownie pack
Returning from St John's.
"See her!" chorus the boys
Returning from nowheremuch.

And there she stares –
Tall
And gaunt
And hair unpinned . . .
Staring
Staring
Staring
Staring beyond the silver slates of Stanley Street
Of Wilmer Way
And distant Arnos Grove.

Head tilted,
As if by mechanical device.
Unmoving,
And unflinching of the handful of gravel
Thrown at her window by the captain of the
    Boys' Brigade.
Always staring.
Never watching,

Always staring.
Staring at her moon.

"Miss Hubbard's moon starin'" bellowed the boy
Who always delivered the classified late.
"Miss Hubbard's moon starin'" echoed the
    Bunyan boys from 43.
And the children gathered,
And the pink fingers pointed,
And the gravel rattled.
And still she stared.

And from the houses the grown ups came –
Nodding
And whispering
And pointing
And murmuring wise things amongst themselves
To lead the children away.

Later that year they also led Miss Hubbard away,
Slowly
And kindly . . .
For staring at the moon.

Gossip
Mango Chutney

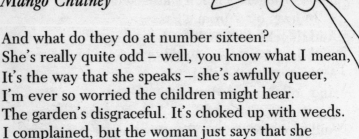

And what do they do at number sixteen?
She's really quite odd – well, you know what I mean,
It's the way that she speaks – she's awfully queer,
I'm ever so worried the children might hear.
The garden's disgraceful. It's choked up with weeds.
I complained, but the woman just says that she
  needs
Every one – and the seeds blow all over the place,
And sprout in our asters. It's a public disgrace!
Enormous weeds, too, quite twenty feet tall,
With bright golden leaves that turn silver and fall
All over the lawn; and flowers like the sun,
Full six feet across; time something was done!

Waiting

Irene Rawnsley

No news isn't good news;
No news nags like toothache
Through six o'clock, seven
When Sandy's not home from school.

No news searches the streets,
Park, supermarket, places where
he could and couldn't be;
Asks everyone.

No news imagines him kidnapped,
Drowned in the canal,
Sleeping rough, beaten up,
Crying to come home.

No news can't eat or think,
Hears twenty times the gate
Click, sees a satchel
Swinging on the kitchen hook.

No news won't go to bed,
Watches the telephone, longs
To spite its silence with
A boy come back tonight.

The tidy burglar
Leo Aylen

The burglar tip-toed across the lawn
That was cut like a carpet, sprinkler-smooth,
Past ornamental waterfall
And pale blue utterly algae-free pool,

Crossed the patio, brushed through vines
Dripping with bunches of ripe, black grapes,
Cracked a window, stepped inside,
Admired the decanters, the velvet drapes,

Examined the stereo, touched the pictures,
Feeling the texture of the jagged oil-paint,
Opened a cabinet with Georgian silver
And Tudor miniatures in intricate frames,

But took nothing. He went upstairs
To the master-bedroom's jewellery cases:
A diamond collar, six rings, a rare
Black pearl, some rubies, a dozen bracelets.

His eye strayed to the rumpled bed.
Untidiness always drove him frantic.
He made it neatly, stacked cushions at the
    head.
Then, hearing a noise, left empty-handed.

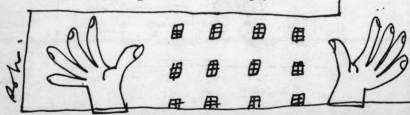

The quick and the dead
John C. Desmond

It is imperative
you remember
the password.
The guards
have orders
to shoot
should any
hesitation
be apparent.

I shall now
demonstrate.
To maintain
authenticity
the guards
will not be
expecting me.

"Good morning."

"Password?"

"Er ——

Micky Hackett's Rocket

Leo Aylen

Mickey Hackett
Built a rocket
From a bracket
And a sprocket.
"Look, Dicky! Book your ticket."
Dicky tried to nick it.
"I'll knock it,
Kick it,
Crack it."
They were making such a racket,
Dad took it,
Tried to pack it
In the pocket
Of his jacket.
But Mick – 'e's quick an' wicked –
Said "Dick, let's see you dock it.
Sneak it out and hook it
To the cooker,
Stick it
Crooked
In the socket,
And tack it."
Wow! What a shock! It
Knocked Dad back. It
Crackled,
Smoked, and blackened
A mackerel,

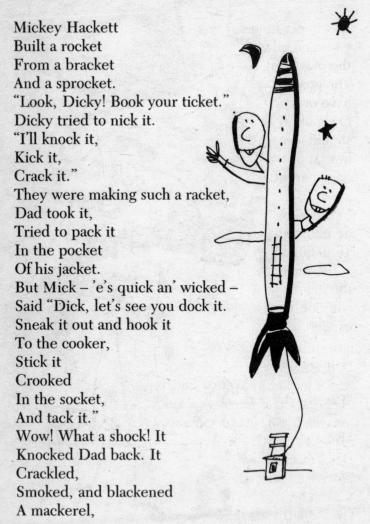

Some cheese crackers,
Dad's mack, a tennis racquet,
And a packet of Mum's stockings.
Mum raised a raucous ruckus,
Smacked 'em, made 'em chuck it
All mucky in the bucket.
Dad whacked 'em,
Thwacked 'em,
Kicked 'em
Up to their room and locked it.

Chuck it

John C. Desmond

"You can get rid of it.
Dirty old thing,
cluttering up your room."

My friend, my
World War One bayonet;
slayer of dragons in the garden,
decimator of pagan hosts,
protector in blackberry jungles.

"Time for your paper round.
Have you mended the puncture?
Take that with you
and dump it."

Stopping at the gravel pits,
tears in my eyes,
I hurled it into the curling mist,
dreading the fatal splash.

Then this hand rose up
and caught it
to sink slowly beneath the surface.

I didn't tell Mum.

Junket
Irene Rawnsley

If something breaks,
a leg drops off or
wheels won't turn or scissors jam
my mum says junket.

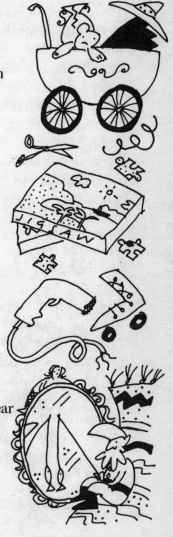

Our garage is a junket store;
baby's pram, jigsaws
with pieces lost,
the hairdryer that won't,
bicycles that would
if somebody troubled to mend
    them,
half a rug my grandmother
grew tired of weaving,
redundant garden gnomes
reflected in a spotted mirror;
junket, all of them.

There came a day when junket
spread too far; my dad
complained he couldn't get the car
inside the garage for junket;
dangerous junket waited
to slash his tyres,
scratch the paint; skates
engaged his feet in the dark;
spokes prodded him.

His anti-junket plan
was launched next evening.

He hired a van to take us
to the tip, death-bed for junket;
forced the doors shut
against the muddle of old tyres,
games, plastic rubbish sacks,
gnomes still smiling bravely
bike wheels singing sad
to be leaving us. Bad,
heaving our familiar junket
into the cold open air,
when we got there.

But dad had his eye
on a cupboard which pleaded
with swinging door
to be noticed. "Two screws
would fix it. It would
keep our junket tidy." Also
we found a sheepskin rug
for the dog's kennel, rope,
garden hose minus rose,
a wobbly chair, two drawers
and a roll of electric flex.

"Amazing," dad told mum
"what people throw away;"
but when he unloaded the van
she said "junket junket junket!"

Dustmen
dave calder

We count the days by shops and alleyways
each bend and length is measured by our shouts
and know the houses by the state of their backgates
the people by whatever they've cast out.

Close to the end of things we heave the reeking
    bins
from paving stone to shoulder with one rising turn
and with the harsh wry humour of gravediggers
we mock the maggots shaken from the metal urn.

In the maze of broken brick and antique
    slippery slabs
where wild potatoes flower and charred tins rust
like hunters we know creatures by their leavings
and view them more with interest than disgust.

Into the wagon's wrecking jaws I've crammed a three-
piece suite, a bedstead, a piano, a dead dog in
    two bits;
slummy goes into the sack, but for a modest fee
we'll crush anything to nothing and drop it in
    the pit.

And every week twenty more tons press on
    four collar bones:
what you throw out lightly falls heavily on us
who bear your past away and bury it, you
    who'll become
worn bones and spoiling meat, old clothes,
    handfuls of dust.

Our playground
Colin West

Our playground wouldn't be so bad
If it didn't slope so much,
But as it is, when we play football,
We have to have two sides:
The Uphills and the Downhills;
And the Uphills always lose.

Life must be as sloping as our playground;
For there always seem two sides:
The Uphills and the Downhills;
And the Uphills always lose.

To Spinney Hill
Oscar Frank

so when to escape
to that grand green park,
seemed like a dream untold,
the leaping heart,
grasped for that moment.
like a ram in its early season,
he'd set off to Spinney
where his friends,
on that stretch of undulating hill
awaited his coming.
then his mind willed
a feeling raw yet exhilarating.
after much anticipation
he stood on the ground,
where many fitful hours
with Santok, Balbur and the rest,
on an uneven pitch
with a football,
they ran their blue bones ragged,
till nightfall
came to call them home
back to their papas and their mums.
then the hot cocoa warmed
their climb up the long stairs
to their beds; and sleep.

Our class
Judith Nicholls

Kevin Nuttall's a dreamer
and Gary Flynn's a fool;
Charlie Watt's the biggest swat
that ever walked in the school.
Put Timmy Fitch on a football pitch
If you want to see him move –
But keep away from Jonathan Grey
        – he's the Guv.

Sally Dee's ginger and freckled
and always good for laughs;
Andy can tell a good story
And Clare's professor of maths.
Marty Stubbs can outstare any teacher –
he's Mary Bollom's love –
but Jonathan Grey always gets his way
        – he's the Guv.

Mike Walder and Annie Bradford
can outrun anyone;
Chris Potts blows the fattest bubbles
on second-hand bits of gum.
Vicki is tough with fist enough
to scare the roughest thug –
but Jonathan Grey they all obey
        – he's the Guv.

Ten little schoolchildren
Trevor Millum

10 little schoolchildren
standing in a line
one opened her mouth too far
and then there were 9

9 little schoolchildren
trying not to be late
one missed the school bus
then there were 8

8 little schoolchildren
in the second eleven
one twisted an ankle
and then there were 7

7 little schoolchildren
trying out some tricks
one went a bit too far
then there were 6

6 little schoolchildren
hoping teacher won't arrive
one flicked a paper dart
and then there were 5

5 little schoolchildren
standing by the door
one tripped the teacher up
and then there were 4

4 little schoolchildren
longing for their tea
one was kept in after school
and then there were 3

3 little schoolchildren
lurking by the loo
teacher saw a puff of smoke
then there were 2

2 little schoolchildren
think that fights are fun
one got a bloody nose
and then there was 1

1 little schoolchild
playing in the sun
whistle blew, buzzer went,
then there were none!

Kung Fu Jean

Lorraine Simeon

Tommy and Jerry the Jackson boys
Never played with girls or toys
They kept their bedroom full of junk
And Tommy said he was a punk

Jerry didn't like to see
Small children playing happily
He'd hide their pram, or kick their ball
Over someone's garden wall

Tommy's hair was blue and grey
He wore the same clothes every day
Playing tricks on everyone
Was his idea of having fun.

A naughty scruffy pair were they
Making children run away
Showing off, acting big
Being mean to little kids.

And then Jean Francis came along
Jean was small but very strong
Jean moved in at number 2
Her favourite hobby was Kung Fu

The Jackson boys thought "Oh how sweet"
They saw Jean skipping down the street
"Let's have ourselves a little joke
And take away her skipping rope"

Tommy was the first to try
But Jean looked him straight in the eye
She spun around, then with a flick
She landed him a Kung Fu kick

"Oi," said Jerry "that's enough
I don't like girls who think they're tough
I'll get you just you wait and see"
But Jean said "You can't frighten me"

Jerry tried to grab Jean's hair
She blocked his move, then jumping clear
She attacked him with her flying jump
And Jerry landed with a thump.

Tommy then said "Let's go home
And leave this little girl alone"
But Jerry thought that Kūng Fu Jean
Was the nicest girl he'd ever seen

So this is how the story ends
The Jackson boys and Jean, are friends
But now it seems the brothers fight
With each other every night

Once they both were rough and mean
But now they're fighting over Jean
Jean likes Tommy – and Jerry too
But most of all she likes KUNG FU

The plot so far
dave calder

With the discovery of the elephants on the roof,
the school was thrown into confusion. Drainpipes
slithered from walls and wriggled away, doors
became unhinged and flew off their handles.
Assembly, that morning, had tasted of custard
and the children, mouths flecked with yellow
    flakes of skin
were having to sit hard to stop their chairs escaping.
Nor could they catch the carrots dangled in
    front of them
for the floor heaved like a sea and the teachers
dropped their fishing rods and clutched at
    desks in seasick panic.
Screams sharp as carving knives stabbed from
    the kitchen
where the elephants, having stamped
a small hole in the leaky ceiling have lowered
their trunks and are kidnapping young cabbages.
The caretaker shouted at them till his back was sore
but they paid no notice and he went to fetch a
    ladder.
The building now started to rock more violently,
the piano in the hall caught fire, a flock
of gutteral parrots swooped along the corridors
or perched in the thickness of twisted creepers
that cascaded urgently through collapsing ceilings.

The desks in the classroom have turned to
    huge, rough stones
but the children lean on them, half-asleep,
for they are warm, as if warmed by the sun,
and the teacher's voice becomes a murmur,
a soft wind among many glossy leaves,
and under the floorboards great fish plunge
in icy darkness: and all the books become trees
and all the chalk becomes earth
and the ink becomes a sluggish, muddy river
where crocodiles crawl in the whirring heat
Meanwhile, the elephants . . .

The space-travellers of Foskett Road Junior School

Leo Aylen

1.
Elton used to dream of flying.

Tuesday break-time
Tracy said she'd show him
Her Harrier ejector-seat.
"That's a stool with a cushion, stupid."
Tracy'd stuck a live wire in it.
Elton leapt up, yelling.
"Told you it was
An ejector seat," said Tracy.

Tuesday night
Elton dreamt he was Superman,
Soaring, swooping, gliding,
Above the skyscrapers,
Up past the moon,
Into outer space,
With Tracy Morgan dangling
Like a wet swim-suit between his fingers.

Wednesday break
Miss made Tracy
Give Elton her iced lolly.

Wednesday night
Elton dreamt Tracy was Lois
Trapped in an earthquake,
And that he
Superman – jetted over the cracking desert . . .
But was . . . just too late to save her.

He woke up grinning,
And had three shredded-wheats for breakfast.

2.
The day the chem-lab in the senior school
    exploded . . .
They found Elton,
His face blackened,
Clutching a bunch of balloons,
And a tattered hosepipe.

"But Miss," he said,
"S'pose I'd bin
First Englishman in space . . ."

This time she thumped him.

"Any'ow," he said defiantly next morning,
"Look! My name's in the papers.
But why do they call me 'Aspirin' Astronaut'?
Not even Tracy Morgan
Says I'm sweaty."

3.
"'Ere! Look at Fatty Simpson's satchel.
It's full of Mars bars."

    "Mars bars makes you fatter
    Than an elephant's bum in batter."

"Wot you doin' in my satchel?
Where's my Mars bars?
I'll shrivel you all to potato-crisps
With my invisible death-ray."

"Mars bars makes you fatter
Than an elephant's bum in batter."

"Fatty cuts 'is Mars bars into slices,
Slips them into 'is corned-beef sandwiches."

"Mars bars makes you fatter
Than an elephant's bum in batter."

"Any'ow, I'm gonna be an astronaut.
So I can eat as many
Mars bars as I like.
'Cause up in space you're weightless.
So there!"

"Mars bars makes you fatter
Than an elephant's bum in batter."

"Mars bars makes you fatter
Than an elephant's . . ."

They've landed
Mike Johnson

They've landed.

Standing at a bus stop
they'll be next to you,
invaders in the queue

(and some of them get half-fare too)

They've landed.

You can easily tell them from us,
because they read "Exchange and Martian".

They've landed.

There's one.

Look closely,
these things are not what they seem;
they are really red and green
and blue;
each hair style's hiding
seven evil eyes,

not to mention antennae . . .

There.
There.

You must believe me.

They've landed.

They've landed.

They've landed.

Jobs
dave calder

I could be

shovelling stars into black holes
or digging the tunnels for government moles
or the first nuclear scientist on the dole

I could be

learning space history from intelligent slime
teaching houseflies to clean up industrial grime
or saving politicians from lives of petty crime

I could be

inventing the rubberised brain-powered car
or sailing a barge down a canal on Mars
or writing HELP large enough to be seen from
  the stars

I could be

a dentist for movie-star sharks
or a social worker for DHSS clerks
or stopping our towns from becoming carparks

I could be
I could be

a survivor under ten tons of lead
a hero (but you have to be dead)
or perfectly happy just staying in bed

I could be

a soldier (but not fire a shot)
a banker (who gives what he's got)
I could be prime minister and not lie a lot

I could be

but I'm not.

High Street Smells
James Kirkup

A busy street is a public library of smells –
the coffee grinder's fresh aroma at the corner,
the baker's sweet, buttery perfume –
you can almost taste the rolls, the pastries,
and drink the toasted coffee on the morning air.

Out of the sweet shops and the candy stores
oozes the exotic scent of marzipan and chocolate,
and the plebeian breath of chewing gum and
    gobstoppers.
The fruit market is a pungent orchard of
    essential juices,
and my ever-wary nose tells me that I'm approaching
the butcher's, with its plain whiffs of blood and
    sawdust,
while the sea itself comes swimming right
    across the pavement
as I pass the fishmonger's briny bouquets in ice
    and salt.

The Chinese takeaway, the Indian curry restaurant,
the fish-and-chip shop, McDonald's (smell is flavour),
the Olde Worlde Teashoppe, all have their
    distinctive auras
and tangs of sweet and sour, poppadums and spice,
deep-drying oil with vinegar. And toast, cakes
    and tea.

A gush of ironing steam from the laundry. The
    dry cleaner's
sharp, stinging reek, like smelling-salts – what
    a pong!
The pubs are open books of beer, wines and spirits
that my nostrils read rapidly, a kind of boozy braille.
The shoe emporium's rich emanations of supple
    leather, new shoes
impregnating the shoe boxes' pure white
    cardboard and tissue paper.
And here's the newsagent's – you can almost
    read the acrid print
of the local weekly, "The Farming World,"
    "The People's Friend,"
"Popular Gardening", and all the comics before
    you even open them!
The voluptuous tobacconist's censes with its
    musky leaf
an entire shopping-mall – the drums, cartons
    and boxes
of honeyed shag, and tins of teasing snuff.

These are just some of the olfactory treats
for the aware nostril, the adventurous nose
seeking, among the banal stink and stench of
    exhaust fumes
the characters, the eccentrics, the silent friends
that are the original fragrances of busy streets.

Missing kissing
Gary Boswell

There's a sign in Boots
saying "Don't share spit

"Don't drink from the bottle
    if there's lipstick on it

"Don't swallow when you're
    swimming
    don't suck the ends of string

"In fact, to be on the safe side,
    DON'T DO ANYTHING."

White lamplight

Gerda Mayer

Why is the night sky rosy at the edges &
over the rooftops?
Is it the breath of lamplight
small and apricot in the distance but,
in the sidestreet here, white,
flowering on tall stalks?

The street of bungalows
takes on a holiday air
it is so at ease.
Its various blunders are hidden.
I sit by the empty milkbottles
under a silken moon
and watch the white lamps flower.

At dawn their petals will drop
leaving stamens of delicate mauve.

cries of london
Wes Magee

the busker and his echoes in the subway
    the fans wild-singing on the train
      the mugged girl weeping in the precinct
        the rain

the marchers and their banner-calls for justice
    the juke-box belting through the bars
      the old jane cursing in the washroom
        the cars

the billboards with their claims and scarlet language
    the crazed drunk yelling out his fears
      the news-stands brash and bold with headlines
        the tears

the dancers as they fall out from the discos
    the weirdo beat up by the boys
      the wet streets filled with feet and voices
        the noise

Accident prone
John C. Desmond

A cable sliced off his head
but brilliant surgery
saved his life.
"Try not to cough",
said the doctor,
"at least till the wound heals."
"Right you are", he nod

ded.

How to open a packet of sandwiches

The final stages of this story shows you trying to open the packet of digestive biscuits. Try not to damage them as your Mum might be mad with you when you get home (..........)

Paul Johnson

Lom remembers
Dave Ward

lom remembers
the old days
back in the old
back street
they called home

where you could
leave your front door
wide open
all day
for people to come & go
as they pleased
& nothing ever got
robbed

"it's not like here"
she says
"here you can put
three locks on your door
& a bolt & chain
& carry a bag full of keys
– still they come
& go through your home
as they please"

"they've taken the telly
& the three-piece suit
& all the photos
of my favourite niece
even the carpet
from under our feet

if they could scrape the wallpaper
off of the walls
they'd take that as well"

lod agrees
"not only that –
but they'd try to sell it you back"

Leaving home
Sandra Mundel

They say them inviting us to England
so we get on a boat and sail to London
there was no sun and the weather well cool
so we stan up in a bush jacket
an a freeze like a fool

Nobody never tell we how
the weather so bad
Nobody never tell we how
De British
them sad

They give we job and de bed fi sleep
Next thing we know them hand
we broom fi sweep

We send go tell we family lie
say we a work for the Queen
as a British Spy

NORTHERN LASS MEETS NORTHERN BLOKE

NICK TOCZEK

HELLO ALL YOU MUMS AND DADS.
SHE'S A RIGHT ONE FOR THE LADS.
FAMOUS PEOPLE TALK MUCH MORE.
I LAID A CARPET ON THE LIVING ROOM FLOOR.
FOUR PINTS OF BITTER, ONE PINT MILD.
MARGARET McCARTHY'S HAD ANOTHER CHILD.
NORTHERN LASS MEETS NORTHERN BLOKE:
TALK, TALK, TALK AND TELL A GOOD JOKE.
SAME OLD ROUTINE EVERY DAY.
LEEDS UNITED RULE - O.K.
SIGNING ON AT NELSON STREET.
YOU'RE THE VERY LAST PERSON I THOUGHT I'D MEET.
HOW'S YOUR ARTHUR? SO'S OUR JACK.
HEY! YOU DON'T HALF LOOK DAFT IN A PLASTIC MAC.
NORTHERN BLOKE MEETS NORTHERN LASS:
TALK, TALK, TALK AND SPEND SOME BRASS.
BINGO QUEUES IN THE BLINDING RAIN.
TORREMOLINOS, THAT'S IN SPAIN.
FISH 'N' CHIPS TO EAT NOW, PLEASE.
I NEVER TOUCH CURRIES, BUT I LIKE CHINESE.
FRIEND OF MINE CAN GET THEM CHEAP
BUT A DROP OR TWO AT NIGHT'LL HELP YOU SLEEP.
NORTHERN LASS MEETS NORTHERN BLOKE:
TALK, TALK, TALK AND YOU END UP BROKE.
SHE KNEW YOU FROM JUNIOR SCHOOL.
SOON AS I WIN THE FOOTBALL POOLS.
TV LICENCE, COUNCIL RENT.
BY WEDNESDAY NIGHT YOU'VE GOT THE WAGES SPENT.
THINGUMMY LOVES WHAT'S-HIS-NAME.
HE, SHE, YOU, ME PLAY THE SAME CLICHÉ LANGUAGE GAME.
NORTHERN BLOKE MEETS NORTHERN LASS:
TALK, TALK, TALK. I SAID TALK, TALK, TALK.
I SAID TALK, TALK, TALK
BUT KEEP IT CRASS.

New signing
Peter Dixon

A star has signed for Liverpool
(or so the papers say)
A mid-field sort of dynamo
(the man who makes the play).
He's number 5, and 6, and 7
He ball wins – strikes and shoots
and tackles like an earth machine
In concrete covered boots.
He hacks, and kicks, and shoots, and yells.
He bellows, trips and slides.
and ankle taps and kneecap raps
and many things besides.
He's filled a thousand caution books.
All refs. can sign HIS name
and when he comes to Liverpool
The game won't be the same!
He'll never pass.
He'll spit and roar
He'll shoot like Al Capone.
A dinosaur of football fields,
a mammoth man of bone.
He cost 2 million pounds they say
and I'm his greatest fan.
I'll watch him play on any day

His name is .... DESPERATE DAN!

Light fingered
John C. Desmond

He shook hands with him
and then with him
and him with her.
They shook hands with us
and we shook hands with them.
You of course shook mine
and I shook his.
Ten minutes later
I realised I had
a hand missing.